The Next Level

Forgiver

Release the Pain

Embrace the Peace

C.L. Holley

DEDICATIONS

To all those whose life is a constant uphill struggle and a consistent battle to find the happiness that once was. May God heal your wounds and restore the good things in your life.

TABLE OF CONTENTS

INTRODUCTION

Years ago, as my older sister and I sat in her living room sharing moments of the past, her bright countenance suddenly lost its glow, and her smile morphed into a frown. Our conversation, which had begun as a happy stroll down memory lane, transformed into a dark moment that shook my soul to the core.

"What's wrong?" I asked.

I waited a few seconds as she attempted to compose herself. She tried to choke back tears but to no avail. They filled her eyes and overflowed down her cheeks. She gently wiped them away and in a somber voice began to share some moments in her childhood of unhealed physical, mental, and emotional scars.

The discussion revolved around the brutality of my father, who was her stepfather. I knew their relationship was strained. She had suffered abuse at his hand, but I never understood the depth of her pain until that moment.

"I was terrified of him, and living with him was like walking on egg shells," she said. "I never knew when he would snap. At times it was little things that seemed to set him off."

I gazed upon the tortured face of a woman in her sixties who apparently, had struggled for over fifty years with painful memories of mistreatment by a man who should have loved and protected her.

Seeing her in that condition made me come to terms with my father's imperfections. He was by most counts a good man and a strong provider for a large family. But he also had a dark side that may have been the result of a difficult life as a sharecropper and the racism of his day. The poverty of farming meant he never owned anything and was often cheated at harvest season.

He lived during the height of the civil rights movement and constantly endured the demeaning injustice of the South. His disdain for whites coupled with a black panther militant mind-set created a man with a dark personality. He could be loving and kind one moment yet instantly violent the next. At times, he showed no mercy during his fits of rage.

It was common for him to become embroiled in terrifying encounters with white neighbors, wheeling a shotgun inches from their faces and threatening to send them to meet Jesus. He was a man who carried a lifetime of deep pain. I believe he never found forgiveness for his personal wounds before his tragic death. I was only five when he passed away.

As my sister continued to release tears, I moved closer to comfort her. In that sobering moment, I realized something about growing up in my family. There were two things that were never said: "I love you" and "I'm sorry, please forgive me."

We loved each other, but those unspoken words could have greatly lessened the hurt we inflicted on one another.

My family's story is not unique. There is no shortage of heartache in the world today. In fact, hurt is something we all know, whether black or white, male or female, rich or poor. To be honest, we live in a world of pain and most of us have experienced a variety of disappointing incidents with which we continue to struggle.

What's your experience? Is it the rejection or abandonment of parents? Their faces should have been the first thing your eyes gazed upon as a newborn. Their voices should have been the first sounds you heard, and their arms the first warmth you felt. Instead, they left you, as if they didn't love or want you, and the pain of rejection is still strong.

You've convinced yourself that you were better off without them and have even made a good life for yourself. But have you overcome the wounds of the past?

Is your experience the violent and senseless killing of a loved one? Whether it occurred through domestic violence, terrorism, or another form, the morbid images and dreadful sights of the incident are seared into your memory. They still haunt you. You know the importance of forgiveness, but have you really walked in it?

Maybe you experienced being abused, raped, or molested. Years later, you continue to mentally lapse back into time to those terrible moments that ripped your soul apart. You try pulling yourself back from the abyss of that memory, but you can hear the person's voice and feel the sickening touch. You know forgiveness is the way out, but have you walked that path of freedom?

Could it be the betrayal by your spouse or significant other? You gave all of your love, time, and commitment only to discover your faithfulness was not returned. When the truth came out, you rode a roller coaster of emotions including shame, hurt, and anger. That was some time ago, and you have reluctantly moved on with your life. But are you truly healed from the nightmare?

Has your experience been racial or religious persecution? They descended upon the group with hateful violence. They killed, tortured, and severely wounded everyone in their path—including those closest to your heart. Years after your imprisonment and release, your soul still searches for solitude from the screams.

Have you hurt someone or even taken a life? Perhaps you've searched and longed for the weight of guilt to be taken away, only to find yourself hard pressed under layers of heartache and regret.

Unfortunately, it's not a matter of if we will have a negative experience; it's a matter of when. That makes perfecting forgiveness extremely important to our well-being.

In fact, I've discovered if we want peace and joy in our lives, we must do one very important thing: forgive. I believe our mental, spiritual, and physical health is directly related not only to forgiving but to what degree we forgive.

As a Christian, I've discovered there are different levels of forgiveness. We can refuse to forgive, forgive a little, or walk on the same level of forgiveness as Jesus Christ walked.

I want to share those levels with you and walk you up the steps, level by level, to the peace and joy found on the highest pentacle of forgiveness.

If you're not a Christian, I invite you to continue reading. In addition to Bible verses and commentary, this book also uses real-life situations with which you can easily identify and relate. I am convinced the stories and examples will be helpful.

The Next Level Forgiver was written as a beacon of hope and healing for those still dealing with the effects of heartache and pain. No, it's not too late to be made whole. Victory is not out of reach or unattainable. It is achievable, possible, and well worth the long journey.

Don't be afraid of the painful emotions and haunting memories. Come take my hand as we start a slow but difficult walk up the steps of freedom and into the marvelous light of peace.

CHAPTER

1

THE BURDEN OF UNRESOLVED HURT

My older brother's routine baffled me. For more than thirty years, I watched him make his way to a large boulder lying on the ground about fifty yards from our house. On sunny days, he perched on the rock like a bird on a tree limb. The view overlooked a small road with a large open field on the other side. Trees and bushes lined the edge of the field to create a peaceful scene.

For hours he sat there, motionless as a statue, only turning his head with the occasional passing of a car. At times, I could see his lips moving as if he were talking to someone or himself. In my early years, I thought those were his times of rest and relaxation. But as I grew older, I had the impression something wasn't right about those long moments of solitude.

To understand my brother's behavior, one needs to understand his history. He was about twenty years older than I, and my only knowledge of his childhood came from older siblings.

"He was a playful and talkative child," my older sister said. "I don't know what happened. As he grew up, he became quiet and began to withdraw from his family."

His adult years were marred with conflict and turmoil. He was in and out of jail, experimented with drugs, and often used alcohol as a sedative for a broken life.

In fact, he was most talkative when intoxicated. That's how I eventually discovered his painful secret from many years earlier. It was something he never dealt with, shared, or came to terms with during his fifty-plus years of living.

One night, after he had consumed several beers, he and I sat in the living room and discussed family history. It was a rare occurrence, so I milked it for all its worth. I put on my interviewer's hat and proceeded to ask questions. I wanted to see further into his past.

"What was your life like growing up during the civil rights movement?"

He leaned back in the chair and took a deep breath as he appeared to collect his thoughts. "Well, most of my life was good."

He went on to share the good times he had as a child growing up in a poor family. He smiled and laughed during some of the recollections. About fifteen minutes into the conversation his facial expression suddenly changed. I could sense something was wrong.

He reached for the beer can beside the chair and turned it up to gulp down the reminder.

13

"I heard a lot about Daddy," I said, trying to rekindle the conversation. "I heard he was a good man but a mean one. I know he wasn't your real daddy, but how did you two get along?"

He stared toward the ceiling. "How old was you when he died?" he asked.

"About five. Was he as mean as people say?"

He hesitated, gazing at the opposite wall of the room. "I'll tell you something I never thought I'd see."

"What?" I asked.

"When I was a little boy—I was somewhere round seven or eight—It was real early in the morning, and I was the only person up in the room. Everyone else was sleep. I was dancing, playing around, and having fun—you know, like kids do. I heard sounds coming from the kitchen. It was next to the room where we slept but the door to our room was closed. It sounded like people wrestling but not fighting because the noise wasn't real loud.

I walked over to the door and peeked through the keyhole, and that's when I saw it."

He stopped talking and sat motionless.

"Saw what? I asked.

He looked at me as if he was trying to decide if he should reveal what he saw. After a few seconds, he spoke. "I saw ..."

What he witnessed was so disturbing and controversial that I choose not to reveal it in this book. To do so would invite strife and turmoil into my family. I don't do this to tease you but to make a point. Every negative event in our lives should be confronted, but not everything should made public.

He had been wrestling with that shocking event for over fifty years.It was then I understood why he sat there day after day talking to himself. I believe he was trying to come to terms with what he saw on the other side of that keyhole.

The people involved in that incident had died years before our conversation, yet he was left holding a huge bag of unanswered questions and raw emotions, including unforgiveness. I wondered what that heavy burden must have felt like.

My brother died a few years later from various health conditions including cancer. I believe unresolved emotions and unaddressed issues led to much of his sickness. Days before his death, I prayed for him to find peace and reconciliation from a lifetime of pain.

What about you? Is there a burden on your shoulder? Is there something or someone you have not confronted or acknowledged? Have you pushed the memories of an uncomfortable event far back into the dark corners of your mind? Have you faced the person who sexually abused, abandoned, or betrayed you? Have you come to terms with the painful emotions of shame, embarrassment, or anger? Have you expressed outwardly the fear and guilt hidden inside? If your answer is no, I only have one solid piece of advice: *You cannot conquer what you refuse to confront.*

The Freedom of Expression

Imagine you are sitting with a group of friends in front of a camp fire. You're having fun roasting marshmallows when you accidently burn your hand in the fire. You immediately yank it

15

away, but the painful sensation surges to your brain. What do you do? What do you say? How do you react?

You need to express the pain and agony of the moment. You scream, shake your hand, and perhaps use a few choice words to reveal your disgust and frustration. You could forcefully hold everything in and pretend the flames didn't hurt. But it takes more energy to conceal your emotions and pain than it does to freely express them.

As humans, our creator gave us the gift of expression because He knew we would experience a wide range of emotions. These emotions were not meant to become captive within the mental walls of our minds. Instead, they were meant to be expressed, shared, and dealt with in a constructive manner.

Expression can be complicated for some of us because we have different personalities. Some of us are introverts who shy away from human interaction—making sharing our hurt more difficult. Still others are extroverts who welcome interaction and have no problems sharing hurtful things.

Regardless of our personality type, we can and should express the hurtful events in our lives instead of attempting to deal with them alone. Here are some methods of expression that people of any personality type can use.

- Private Journal
  Writing could be a great way of transferring your thoughts and emotions from your mind onto paper or electronic device. This may help you think through the events, formulate new or different opinions. It may also benefit

you to read what is written—allowing you to become more familiar with your own viewpoint.

- Confide in Someone You Trust
  You can talk to someone you trust such as a counselor, priest, or pastor. This is a great way to get the secret outside of yourself and receive advice on how to process those hurtful memories and emotions.

- Lovingly Confront the Person
  Caution and wisdom must be used in doing this. If the person is still alive, it may be necessary to bring hidden events out into the open. Depending on the possible volatility of the situation, it may be wise to take a person along with you for protection and to intervene if things become too heated.

  The ultimate goal of confronting a person should be to reconcile, not merely dump out years of hurt and pain.

You can use one or more of these expressions. You can begin with a private journal, proceed to confide in someone, and when the time is right, lovingly confront the person. One thing is certain: before you can achieve forgiveness, you must first acknowledge that the painful event happened and express all the negativity that came along with it through one or all of the methods discussed.

Remember, you cannot overcome what you refuse to confront. Are you ready to overcome? Are you ready to take the power away from those haunting memories and emotions?

CHAPTER

2

LEVEL ZERO – I WILL NOT FORGIVE!

The year 2001 brought tremendous blessings to our household. My wife, Cassandra, and I enjoyed great relationships with each other and with our two children, thirteen-year-old Torrell and eight-year-old Kiana.

The Lord blessed me with a great position with an influential healthcare organization, and I was financially able to purchase our first home. It was the home of our dreams—a beautiful bright-yellow and hunter-green two-story house with a huge backyard. As a family, we played baseball and football in the backyard and the kids joyfully jumped on the large trampoline.

Our devotion to the Lord was the pinnacle of these blessings. I had been called into the ministry one year earlier and my personal relationship with God grew tremendously. Prayer, study, and fasting became an integral part of my life. As a result, there were times when I could clearly hear God's voice and sense His presence. I was in awe of what the Lord was doing in me and in my life.

During the early part of 2001, Torrell and Kiana accepted Jesus Christ as their Lord and Savior. My entire household was saved. At times during the night, as our children slept, I kneeled beside their beds and prayed over them—declaring their futures to be bright and their lives to be dedicated to the work of the Lord.

I wondered if life could get any better. It only took one day, one phone call, and one tragedy to shatter it all. On Friday, October 19, 2001, our blessed household came tumbling down in an instant.

It was around five p.m., and I was walking in a department store with several items in my hand, mentally rehearsing my sermon message for the upcoming Sunday. When I answered the phone, I heard a hysterical voice that sounded like my wife.

"Honey," I interrupted, "please calm down. I can't understand you."

She took a deep breath and repeated, "The school called. Torrell had an accident during basketball tryouts, and it's serious. The ambulance rushed him to the hospital. We need to meet them there as soon as possible."

"Okay," I said, hurrying toward the door."I will pick up you and Kiana."

The atmosphere in the car was stone silent during most of the twenty-five-minute drive to the hospital. Thoughts of fear and anxiety filled our minds. I broke the silence and shared words of hope and inspiration.

I took Cassandra's hand and smiled. "Don't worry, everything is going to be oaky. We have to trust in God and believe Torrell's needs will be met."

We arrived at the hospital and were escorted down a hallway and around a corner where we saw Torrell's basketball coach leaning against a wall. His head was down and tears covered his cheeks."How is Torrell?" I asked.

He looked at me and hesitated. "It don't look good," he said. "The doctor will tell you more."

We located the doctor, and he escorted us into a small private room. We all held onto each other in anticipation of the news. "Doctor," I said. "What's the problem? How is he?"

He took a deep breath and said, "Mr. Holley, I'm so sorry, but your son didn't make it."

My heart skipped beat, and my knees buckled."What do you mean didn't make it? Are you saying our son is dead?"

He took another breath and softly repeated , "I'm so sorry."

We all broke down crying as we tightly gripped each other for comfort. In the midst of the crying, little Kiana spoke words that broke my heart, "I won't have anyone to play with anymore."

As we continued to cry and hold each other, I looked up and mentally scolded God. I trusted you, and you let me down! I'll never forgive you for this!

The coaches and teachers eventually came and explained what happened. By their account, Torrell was running down the court and suddenly collapsed. To them, it appeared to be cardiac related, but they weren't sure why it happened. After speaking with the ER doctor and nurse on staff, we requested an autopsy.

Hours later, after viewing Torrell's body, we finally managed to leave the hospital and make the long drive home. That night, we all curled up together in the same bed and cried ourselves to sleep.

Three weeks later, Cassandra expressed her emotion of anger. "Somebody should have done something to save my son's life!"She broke down into tears. To her, someone was to blame and she entertained accusations toward several people involved in the incident. I could see the devastating effect of the resentment that filled her thoughts. She spent more and more time hiding in a dark bedroom behind closed curtains. She often rehearsed and nursed the bitterness.

Nothing could ease the pain or provide the peace she so desperately needed. On a cold winter's day, weeks after our son's burial, she stood in front of our bedroom window with her hand resting on the glass. "I wonder if he's cold," she whispered, her voice lifeless..

I starred at her and wondered what I should say. Finally, I spoke up and tried to reassure her, "He's not cold. He's just fine."

She saw doctors and took medications, but none of it helped. She sank into deep depression and even entertained thoughts of taking her own life. I felt helpless as her husband and even guilty because I couldn't give her what she needed to get better.

While she struggled with anger and blame, I waged the war of faith. I didn't blame God for our son's death, but I was angry with

Him for not performing a miracle to save his life. I accused Him of not caring about my family and felt betrayed. I had memorized many biblical promises of good health and protection but surmised that none of them were true. I entertained a haunting thought, *How could I have believed in a fairy-tale God who doesn't exist?*

Cassandra and I were sinking fast into a sea of resentment. I wanted answers and reassurance. She wanted those she felt responsible to be held accountable. Neither of us received what we wanted. It was the darkest and most miserable time of our lives.

***

Can you identify with any of the emotions, thoughts, and struggles we faced? Where are you concerning your tragedy? Have you overcome the crippling sense of despair from the sexual abuse, rape, or molestation? Have you conquered the anger that captured your heart when your loved one was violently and senselessly murdered? Have you dealt with the shame of the betrayal from the person you once trusted and loved with all your heart? Have the haunting questions been answered about the abandonment of those who should have loved, cared for, and protected you?

Anger, confusion, and bitterness tend to create an introverted, selfish viewpoint that constantly asks the question, *Why me?* In my opinion, the most miserable place to be is locked in a mental prison with one's thoughts totally focused on self—allowing no one else in and refusing any constructive assistance. I call it a Pity Party Room where we symbolically lounge around on the victim's sofa and meditate on the unfairness of it all—constantly repeating, *Why me?*

That's where my wife and I were, in the Pity Party Room. We were locked up within the tiny confines of our own minds—loathing that the tragedy had to happen to us. *Why Torrell?* we asked. *He was a good boy.*

We were stuck on Level Zero forgiveness. I call this Level Zero because it is the lowest level possible. A person stuck on this level has not forgiven and has chosen to live with the misery of unresolved hurt and anger. This often happens because of a misunderstanding of forgiveness or the belief that what happened is too traumatic to forgive. Yes, some things are harder than others to forgive, but biblically speaking, nothing is too traumatic to forgive. Why? Because God gives us the power to forgive and to overcome all the negative emotions we may be experiencing.

Therefore, a refusal to forgive equates to making these statements:

I refuse to forgive and be healed.

I refuse to humble myself and be exalted

I refuse to release others from their debt and be freed.

I refuse to be forgive and be forgiven of my sins.

Do these statements make sense to you? If not, then why not forgive and receive all the benefits that forgiveness brings? Is it hatred that's stopping you? Is it bitterness that has taken you hostage and is keeping you held in a place of mental and emotional torment? Do you want to be released from the anger, or do you want revenge more than you want peace?

Self-Examination: Level Zero Forgiveness

How do I view the person?

I see him or her as my sworn enemy and my thoughts of that person are those of harm. I crave revenge in the most painful way possible. The sight of my enemy controls me in that his or her presence fills me with anger and hatred.

What am I obeying?

I am obeying my negative thoughts and emotions. At times, I can hear a small voice say, *Forgive, and let it go.* But the voices of revenge, hatred, and bitterness are much louder. I choose to follow the loud voices and feel enslaved to them. I want the person to feel what I've felt, experience whatI've experienced, and hurt like I've hurt.

Where is my focus?

My focus is self-centered. I'm consumed with thoughts of my hurt, my pain, and my negative experiences. I remain lodged in a place of immobility. I cannot move outside my own thoughts.

Where is my relationship with God?

It is strained. There is a barrier between God and me. He wants me to forgive and experience the joys of forgiveness. He gives me grace and time to do what is right, and He knows the battle taking place in my heart, soul, and mind. He loves me, but He also expects me to forgive.

CHAPTER

3

LEVEL ONE – I FORGIVE, BUT I'M DONE!

Have you ever said or heard someone say, "I forgive you, but I'm done with you"?

I was in that place after the death of my son. Months after his passing, I sat motionless on the sofa at five a.m. I mulled over a question that haunted me—Charlie, where are you in your relationship with the Lord?

I picked up the cup of coffee, sipped, and began to survey my life. I attempted to pinpoint the exact place or time when a once-joyful and vibrant relationship with my heavenly Father had fallen into a dull and unfulfilling ritual.

I returned to preaching and teaching only a few weeks after the tragedy, and now I entertained the possibility that it had been too soon. Perhaps I needed more time to mourn, think, and resolve some issues. I returned more out of duty than of a passion and desire to share the Word of God. I knew there were people counting on me to demonstrate my faith and trust in the Lord. They wanted to see me live the faith, and I didn't want to disappoint them.

Therefore, I climbed the pulpit steps each Sunday and proclaimed the Gospel with power. I taught Bible study lessons Wednesday nights and imparted truths of the Word with the wisdom of the Spirit. Someone said, "I know Charlie is going to be all right. No one can preach like that unless God is with him."

That person wasn't aware of my emptiness. I could preach and teach because I was called and gifted by God, but when those responsibilities were finished, I sank right back into a dark and gloomy world of depression. My actions were a way of saying to God, "I'm ready to move forward with your will, but from this point on, our relationship is strictly business. I forgive you, but I'm done seeking intimacy with you, and I'm done believing in your promises."

It was foolish to think I could do the work of God while keeping my distance from Him. The self-conviction of preaching and teaching took its toll, and I was often convicted by my own words. In my heart, I longed for the intimacy of the past with the Lord. I missed the incredible peace and joy that accompanied trust in Him. The burden of an empty soul became too much for me, and that quiet morning on my sofa, I surrendered.

I prayed:

"Father, I'm so angry, confused, and hurt. I feel betrayed and abandoned by you. I don't understand how you could allow such a horrible thing to happen to us. But despite what I feel or think, in my heart I know you love us. Please forgive me for all the unholy things I said to you and about you. According to your tender mercies, remove my guilt and restore the peace of your presence. Please come into my life, and carry me through this."

As I continued to pray, cry, and meditate, I could sense a spiritual restoration occurring within me. In my sanctified imagination, I could hear the Lord's response to my prayer:

"Charlie, I know your pain and I feel your hurt. The only assurance I can give you at the moment is I love you and I'm here for You."

Those words were enough to restore peace to my tormented soul. I wiped away tears and repeated the words of proverbs 3:5-6:

"Trust in the Lord with all your heart,

And lean not unto your own understanding;

In all your ways acknowledge Him,

And He shall direct your paths."

Can You Identify?

Have you ever extended someone conditional forgiveness as I did with God? In other words, I said, "Lord, I forgive You, but our relationship will never be the same."

How arrogant of me. Fortunately, God doesn't take every word we say seriously. He knows when we speak from hurt and bitterness and offers grace and mercy instead of instant judgment.

Have you ever spoken the words of forgiveness yet pushed someone completely out of your life—vowing never to love or trust them again? Do you have an estranged relationship that needs to be repaired?

In situations such as rape and abuse, there may be justifiable reasons to keep a person at arm's length. However, there may be past good relationships that were interrupted by the hurtful actions of one or both parties. Instead of forgiving, repairing, and restoring, the relationship abruptly ended with the words, "I'm done with you!"

Here are some questions to ask and answer if you're trying to decide what to do about a fallen relationship.

- Will a good relationship with this person fill a void I have?

- Is this a relationship worth having and would it enhance my life?

- Is this a relationship I should have?

Your answer to these questions will reveal if it's a relationship that you should pursue, but it will take lots of humility and grace from the Lord to move forward.

Why is forgiveness so difficult?

It would help us to understand what we are up against when it comes to forgiveness. The more we comprehend about this struggle, the more likely we are to overcome. Let's discuss factors that may contribute to a lack of forgiveness.

We fail to deal with the hurt

Example: When they told Sophia about the accident, she felt in her heart that her three children were dead. Three years later, there was still a mountain of hurt associated with that tremendous tragedy. And now, on Mother's Day, the pain had become so intense that it seemed too much for her to handle.

***

It's natural to avoid unpleasant things. We may not want to come face-to-face with the powerful emotions attached to an incident. Those crippling feelings of helplessness, shame, and embarrassment tend to be too overwhelming to sort through. But as Sophia discovered, failing to deal with the hurt can cause a buildup of pain. Perhaps she needed to become involved in a grief support group. Perhaps she needed to talk with someone going through a similar situation. One thing was certain—like all of us, Sophia needed to usher those dominating issues, as painful as they were, to the surface. If not, she was doomed to a life of unresolved feelings that robbed her of peace and joy. Have you stood toe-to-toe with and faced the unpleasant incidents in your life?

We misunderstand forgiveness

Example: Marvin sat in the grief support group with his mind elsewhere. Today was the fourth anniversary of the robbery and brutal murder of his loving wife of fourteen years.

"Group, I know it's a difficult thing to do," the grief counselor said, "but today we are going to discuss how forgiveness plays a role in our grieving process.".

Marvin stared at the counselor and mumbled,"I'll die and go to hell before I let that murderer off the hook!"

***

Misunderstandings about forgiveness can leave us chained to anger and hatred. Marvin needed someone to explain that forgiveness doesn't let those who hurt us off the hook. Forgiveness does not mean what the person did doesn't matter. The effects are real. The nightmares, constant flashbacks, and confusion often become entrenched in our minds and lead to a life of struggle. Forgiveness alone will not erase these powerful occurrences. But forgiveness will free us from the negative impacts to make room in our hearts and minds for healing. When we forgive others, we set the stage for our release from bondage. When we say, "I forgive you," it equates to saying, "I forgive you, and I release me."

Forgiveness involves a long process

Example: Steven couldn't understand why he continued to feel hatred toward his ex-wife. After all, it had been years since she left him for another man while showering her lover with gifts funded from his bank account. Now, she professed to be a born-again believer in Christ, even apologizing for her past actions. Steven had followed the path of forgiveness but wondered if he really had forgiven.

***

Steven discovered something not many people are aware of: Forgiveness involves a long process. For some, it may become a lifelong process. In this microwave-minded generation, it's not easy to become engaged in anything that's long and drawn out. Yes, Stephen had granted forgiveness to his ex-wife years ago, but he wasn't aware it would take many more years to work through the crippling emotions. It was a long path he did not anticipate.

Once we grant forgiveness, we must live in a manner that reflects forgiveness toward others. This includes constant prayer and asking God to grant wisdom and a change of heart. It becomes a process, and this process can be an extensive and difficult journey.

How long have you had undesirable emotions?

We see our shortcomings as small compared to others'

Example: Alvin gazed at the television set but wasn't interested in the show. When his wife asked what was wrong, he said,"Nothing. It's nothing."

He didn't want to go into it at the moment. In fact, he managed to avoid the subject for their entire marriage.

Alvin didn't want her to know about his deadbeat dad who left Alvin's mother and four children to struggle for themselves while he had the time of his life. Alvin rarely heard from him and held only contempt and hatred for him. He longed to experience the relationship of a true father.

***

We may easily become angry and frustrated with the sins and shortcomings of others while downplaying our own. Alvin's father deeply wounded him, and Alvin could clearly see his father's mistakes. But had Alvin carefully considered his own?

It becomes difficult to grant forgiveness if we have a holier-than-thou attitude. In painful situations, we have every right to be hurt or angry, but we don't have the right to be judgmental. Forgiveness is highly unlikely if we remain in this dangerous frame of mind.

We have not matured enough in our love for Christ.

Example: Crystal stared at the mother of the drunk driver who killed her daughter. As the judge pronounced the sentence, the mother's anguish provided Crystal with a moment of satisfaction. Yes, Crystal knew Christ, but she wanted the mother of her child's murderer to feel the hurt and pain she had been carrying for several years.

Crystal thought, I want her to see how it feels to drown in grief.

***

Christians have a tremendous responsibility as followers of Christ. In several ways, Jesus equated obedience to Him as love for Him. He said if we love Him, we will be obedient to Him. He instructs us to forgive, and if we really love Him enough, that love will become the driving force behind our forgiving.

In Crystal's case, her hatred and bitterness about the death of her daughter had overshadowed her love for Christ. Instead of seeking to do the thing that pleased her Lord and Savior, she sought to fulfill her own desire for revenge. Simply put, willful disobedience results from a lack of love for Jesus.

Misconceptions of forgiveness

Misunderstandings of forgiveness can also keep us bound. Let's examine and correct a few of the widely accepted misconceptions.

I must wait until I am no longer angry before I forgive.

Forgiveness is not emotional (something we do based on how we feel). We should not wait until all anger and ill feelings disappear before we consider forgiving.

Instead, we should voluntarily engage in the necessary acts that lead to forgiveness despite the emotional backlash.

Pain and anger cannot be dealt with until forgiveness is first addressed.

Jesus, the ultimate example, demonstrated this act. They beat Him, spat on Him, and put a crown of thorns on His head. They marched Him up a rugged hill, and hung Him in the blistering sun, nailed to a wooden cross. Yet, before He died, He spoke words of forgiveness from the cross.

We can conclude forgiveness does not rely on our emotions. Therefore, we need not wait for anger and hatred to disappear before forgiving.

Forgiving means those who hurt me won't be punished.

We may view our forgiveness as free pass from justice for those who hurt us. That's not the case. Our forgiveness doesn't belittle or lessen the importance of the offense. Neither does it remove the need for justice and recompense.

The wounds of the incident are deep, and the pain is real. Forgiveness does not mean it was no big deal or suggest the entire occurrence should be forgotten or swept under the rug. It is possible to forgive yet continue to seek justice for wrongs committed.

I can forgive when I'm ready. I have plenty of time.

One of the most dangerous parts to play is that of a casual forgiver. We may look for limits and time frames for forgiveness. The longer we live without forgiving, the longer our mental, emotional, and physical condition will suffer. Also, the longer we refuse to forgive, the longer we postpone our healing.

There weren't many things Jesus instructed Christians to do quickly, but forgiving was one of them. He said,

"Settle things with your adversary quickly, do it while you are on the way." (Matthew 5:25)

Healing should never be postponed or delayed. The time is now.

I must forget if I truly forgive.

We are blessed with something wonderful called remembrance. Our minds have the ability to recall incidents of the past, bad and good.

Wouldn't it be wonderful if we could somehow program our minds to remember only the good? We would be able to conveniently forget all the heartaches and pains.

Have you ever tried to forget something? For most people, the more they try to forget, the more that situation comes to mind. Try as we might, we cannot forget the horrible things that happened in our lives. But our recollection need not be wiped out before we accomplish forgiveness.

I have a few scares from various accidents during childhood. I can still remember how they came about, but the pain associated with them is gone. They have healed.

This principle holds true with forgiveness. We may never forget, but if we properly address it—like a natural wound—the pain should grow weaker and weaker.

Perfect Forgiveness Comes from the Heart.

Jesus says we should forgive from the heart. What does that mean? The heart in New Testament Scripture partially means the mind, emotions, and will. These are three powerful areas of our being that must be in agreement if we are to successfully forgive.

The mind contains the memories of the incident—what was said and done, and how and when it happened. The emotions are the feelings that resulted—the hurt, anger, and shame that settled into our being and became a part of our lives. The will is the determination to do something about it as opposed to cover up. It's the will that reaches the conclusion that something must change.

If you're on level zero, have you determined in your mind and will that something must change? Are you tired of carrying the pain and avoiding discussion on the subject that changed your life? Do you have the will to move forward and through the many emotions that will resurface?

If your answer is yes, here are some forgiveness principles to practice.

Say I forgive you from the heart.

Speak with sincerity and with an honest intention to follow the disciplines of forgiveness no matter how you feel. When you fall short or violate one of the disciplines, quickly acknowledge it, ask God for forgiveness, and move on.

Say who you forgive and what you forgive.

It's very important to speak the details of who and what. That may involve bringing up some hurtful memories and emotions, but it is necessary to receive healing. Here are some examples:

- I forgive my parent, _____,for rejecting me, abandoning me, and never being in my life.

- I forgive my relative, _____, for sexually abusing me when I was a child.

- I forgive my spouse, ____, for betraying my trust and sleeping with another person.

- I forgive ____, the person who murdered my loved one and took someone very important from me.

Yes, it will hurt and be very difficult. But we should be as detailed as we can with what we are willing to confront.

Release the person from any debt they owe you.

There are times when we may wait on the person to apologize or make amends for what they've done. In a perfect world, they should. However, our healing should not rely upon their actions. Instead, our healing will come from our actions. Here is an example of a freedom declaration:

I hereby release my father from anything he owed me. He does not owe me an apology, an explanation, or any attempt to make up for what he did. I cancel his debt and set him free from my expectations.

Seek justice, not revenge.

There are situations that require justice. Forgiveness does not forgo the need for proper punishment. Therefore, it is right to seek justice if a crime has been committed. However, we should not set out to aid justice by taking things into our own hands. We should not seek to harm, in any way, the person who hurt us. Instead, we should leave justice to the governing system set in place to administer the punishment. Here is a declaration of justice:

I will not seek revenge—to hurt or harm or repay in any way. Instead, I will put my trust in God and the system to administer justice.

Don't embarrass the person in front of others.

The more we speak about that person in a bitter way, the more anger and pain remain ingrained in us. What we speak with our mouths ultimately comes from our hearts. Saying bitter and hateful things means we have bitterness and hatred deep within. Earlier, we discussed the importance of forgiving from the heart (mind, will, and emotions) which cannot be filled with bitterness and forgiveness at the same time. We must relinquish one of the two and it all begins with words.

Example: Rhonda sat in the divorce hearing fighting back tears. The hurtful lies coming from her ex-husband cut her soul to pieces.

How could someone who said they loved her try to ruin her life?

She knew the truth. She was the one who tried everything to keep the marriage together. She looked the other way after discovering his many affairs. She worked a second job to feed and clothe their children after he was fired.

She even tolerated physical and mental abuse for years. And after all that, he had the nerve to slap her with a notice of divorce and engage in a battle to take their children away.

At the first break in the hearings, Rhonda's best friend escorted her out of the building and into the fresh air. "I know it really hurts you to hear those lies coming from someone you once loved, but I want you to forgive him for all the awful things he has done to you and your children," her friend said.

"No way!" Rhonda burst forth. "I want him to feel all the hurt I'm feeling! I want him to pay ten times over for destroying this family and trying to take my kids! There is no way I'm going to forgive him and let him off the hook!"

Rhonda's friend slowly pulled her close and warmly embraced her. "I didn't say that to let him off the hook. I said it so you can free yourself."

Rhonda frowned.

Her friend continued. "Look at what the anger and bitterness is doing to you. It's destroying your whole life. You can't sleep at night, your health is failing, and your children notice the change in your behavior toward them."

She continued. "Forgiveness doesn't let him off the hook, but

C.L. HOLLEY

it does set you free. Please don't destroy yourself along with him. You must learn to forgive."

As they embraced again, Rhonda finally understood her situation. She knew her friend was right. She needed relief from the inner wars and battles of bitterness and anger. Rhonda stared into her friend's eyes, "I need to forgive, but I don't know how. Please help me."

Rhonda's friend extended her hands, "Just repeat this prayer with me:

Father, you know how much I've been hurt through all of this, and you know the hurt of my children. Father, I'm asking you to forgive him, not because I want to but because you said to forgive. I pray that you will remove all of this anger and hurt inside of me and help me to love my enemies. I receive your peace, comfort, and joy into my heart this very second. In Jesus' name, amen."

They both remained silent for a few minutes and allowed God to touch Rhonda's heart. Rhonda sensed the peace of God as her tears flowed. At the restart of the hearing, Rhonda's face wore a different expression: one of peace and contentment. Rhonda had found the secret to freeing herself from anger and bitterness. That secret was forgiveness.

***

As Rhonda discovered, her biggest fight was with her emotions. But her friend helped her address the negatives of what she was feeling while asking God to heal her from the wounds. Have you asked God to deal with those damaging emotions inside you?

39

Self-Examination: Level One Forgiveness

Where is My Focus?

Level 1 forgiveness indicates my focus has changed from my hurt to my healing. The hurt is still painful, but I realize the need for something to change. I don't desire to continue on the same path, so I take the step necessary for healing. I forgive. Not because I desire it, but because I need freedom.

How do I see the offender?

I still see the offender through eyes and thoughts of bitterness. My desire, at times, is for revenge and my will is for my offender to suffer and to experience all the negatives they've brought upon me.

How is My Relationship with God?

The barrier between God and me was removed the moment I spoke the words of forgiveness. God and I now enjoy a peaceful relationship and He is free to help me overcome the many emotions I'm struggling with.

What's controlling me?

I'm finally overcoming emotional control and heeding the call of the Word of God. The command of Jesus to forgive is the controlling factor in my life.

How do I move to the next level?

I must change my viewpoint of my offender.

CHAPTER

4

LEVEL TWO – I PRAY FOR YOU, BUT STAY AWAY

D ays after my prayer and confession on the sofa, my day-to-day struggle with emptiness began to dissipate. It was easier to read and meditate on the Word of God. I felt unhindered as in times past, and prayer felt natural as my words flowed to the Lord. The vibrant and fulfilling fellowship with my heavenly Father was returning, and for that I was ecstatic. But my wife, Cassandra, still struggled.

I remained very concerned about her physical, emotional, and spiritual condition. I constantly prayed and asked the Lord to remove the invisible blanket of depression that covered her mind, give her answers to painful questions, and help her see the need to live and love again. Day by day and little by little, I saw small improvements in her demeanor and tone which made me hopeful for a full recovery. As we talked at bedtime, I decided to share another point of view.

"You know," I said. "One of the things I was angry with God about was His inaction during our son's death. I accused Him of not caring enough to do something. I know He could have saved our son's life regardless of what others did or didn't do."

She slowly turned her head toward me and muttered, "Really?"

"Yeah," I continued. "We weren't there, but I can't imagine what the coach and teammates went through. It must have been horrible to witness his passing. I remember the expression on the coach's face when I saw him at the hospital. I believe he may be carrying guilt for not being able to save Torrell even though he did the best he could.I don't think we are the only people hurting from this. I've been praying for them too."

I could see something in her eyes that I had not seen in months: life. I believe she was really thinking about my words. After a few moments of Chapter 9: silence, she took my hand and gently caressed it. I took that as an acknowledgment that she agreed.I believe from that moment forward she, too, began to pray for the coach and Torrell's teammates.

In time, Cassandra slowly came out of isolation and withdrawal, even returning to reading her Bible. But she resisted and limited any direct contact with Torrell's coaches and teammates. I noticed that she was very tense and irritable whenever we attended an event honoring our son.

"What's wrong? I asked during one of the events.

"I don't want to be here," she responded. "Let's get this over with and leave as soon as possible."

"Okay." I said.

As we rode home one night, she shared why she never looked forward to those events.

"Every time I see one of them," she said, "it brings all those hurtful memories right back. I don't want to deal with that right now."

"Yes," I said, "I understand. Next time I can go alone."

I believe she had forgiven them for the things she thought they should have done, but she had associated their presence with the pain of the tragedy. She wanted to avoid that by avoiding them. I didn't know how to help her past that mental association.

I also believe she recognized their need to be comforted and encouraged, but she could not bring herself to serve as that comforter or encourager.

I decided to keep her lifted in prayer as I asked the Lord to touch her heart and transform her mind.

Can you identify with Cassandra's experience? Have you separated yourself from the person who hurt you? Perhaps you realize that person's need, but you may be unwilling or unable to become directly involved in providing that assistance.

If you were able to move to level-two forgiveness, you acknowledge that your perpetrator is a person who lacks something vital in life. It may be a lack of:

- Moral values: the basic knowledge of right and wrong.

- Self-control: the ability to resist harmful impulses and thoughts.

- Commitment: the will to be there for you no matter what.

- Character: exemplifying reliability and trustworthiness.

- Mental or emotional soundness: having psychological and emotional wellness and good judgment.

- Love and compassion: genuine care and concern for others.

Have you heard the saying "Hurting people hurt other people"? I believe this to be true. The same person who brought much pain to your life is the same person with pain in his or her life. What could that person's pain be?

- The sting of rejection or abandonment?

- The pain of abuse or molestation?

- The burden of loneliness?

- The load of hatred and anger?

Is it possible the rapist may have been raped or molested? Is it possible the abuser could have been beaten or attacked? Is it possible the unfaithful partner could have been forsaken and never felt connected to anyone? Can you see beyond what was done to you and into the root issue with that person?

What is their root problem? What is he or she missing? Why are you separating yourself?

There are situations where separation may be legitimate. It may be wise to avoid contact with someone who raped, molested, or abused you—especially if that person shows no signs of remorse and refuses to acknowledge or accept responsibility. However, there are broken relationships that were good and are worth the pursuit.

Do you have damaged or broken relationships that should be repaired? Do you pray for or wish certain persons well from afar because it is too difficult to come into their presence?

One of the reasons humans tend to struggle in this area is because we are beings of association. We mentally link occurrences with images, sounds, and experiences. Thus, when we have a bad experience, we make mental association between that experience and the persons involved. The survivor of the murdered is mentally linked to the murderer, the abused to the abuser, and the theft victim to the thief.

There is no way known to man to unlink or disassociate these mental connections with our experiences. Are we doomed to live the rest of our lives with the heartache and painful memories lurking in our minds? Will it always be difficult to approach the offender, make peace, and move forward to establish a meaningful and healthful relationship? How can we break those haunting associations?"

One key can be found in the Christian faith. The Scriptures teach that God looks beyond the faults of humans and sees their needs. Instead of condemnation, He sees below the surface of their actions and deep into the reasons of their behavior—offering mercy and grace. His purpose is restoration and redemption. Perhaps, that should also be our purpose toward perpetrators.

Self-Examination: Level Two Forgiveness

Where is My Focus?
I realize my experience is a triangle between God, the offender, and me. I'm beginning to look beyond my hurt and see the need of the person who committed the act, but I'm unwilling to become directly involved in providing that need.

How do I see the offender?
Because of the mental association with the experience, thoughts, memories, and painful emotions surface whenever I see the person. I offer up a prayer and even wish some good would happen to that person, but I'm not ready for a direct, face-to-face encounter.

How is My Relationship with God?
I'm growing in the Lord and beginning to see the offender as God does—through the eyes of mercy and in need of help. I'm asking God to help move past the mental associations to do what I know He wants me to do: reach out to the offender and demonstrate true love, forgiveness, and compassion.

What's controlling me?
Although the pain of the experience is keeping me from reaching out, my desire to please the Lord is growing stronger. I have confidence that soon God will give me the power, courage, and opportunity to make contact with my offender.

How do I move to the next level?
The negative mental associations cannot be removed, so I must weaken their effect by building new positive associations with the offender.

CHAPTER

5

LEVEL THREE - I FORGIVE AND REACH OUT

I t was one of the most powerful displays of true remorse I had ever seen. After Torrell passed, teammates and schoolmates wrote hundreds of letters—boxes and bags filled with personal notes, drawings, and cards with heart-touching condolences.

They were like a treasure chest with priceless jewels. Some described qualities in ways I had never known or imagined. Others relayed funny stories and experiences with him. But the ones that affected me most where those written by the students who bullied him.

A year before Torrell died, they made his school experience very difficult. They teased, tormented, and even physically attacked him on more than one occasion. I spoke to the school principal, and Cassandra and I constantly talked to him and tried to extend comfort and encouragement. But through it all, I believe the weight of the harassment drove him into depression and anger.

I knew who they were, and I shamefully admit that, for a time, I hated them for bringing that pain into his life. After Torrell's death, my hatred transformed into utter contempt. I managed to mask the bitterness behind a smile whenever I came into contact with one of them. It wasn't until I read their letters that I began to see their hurt and regret. I became convicted of my hatred, and my heart filled with sorrow for them. Their apologies written on paper seemed genuine. In a way, I could feel their pain and remorse.

One of them wrote, "I didn't treat you like you deserved…that I will forever regret."

Another wrote, "I'll never be mean to anyone else again."

Cassandra and I often retired to Torrell's room, grabbed a handful of letters, and soaked in the warm words and incredibly talented illustrations. To me they were therapy, and I believe Cassandra used them in the same way. Some brought tears to our eyes; others made us laugh. Many gave us more insight into our son's life and interactions with his schoolmates.

At times, we discussed the letters and shared our thoughts and emotions from certain cards—including the ones written by the students who bullied our son.

The more letters we read, the more change I saw in Cassandra's attitude and mind-set toward those students. Over time, she expressed less criticism and anger toward them. I noticed when she came in contact with those students she shared her experience with depression and encouraged them in several ways. I can't pinpoint an exact date or time it all happened, but I can say the wall she had placed between herself and them eventually came down. She began to interact with and reach out to them in a loving, kind, and compassionate manner.

I believe the letters and cards helped her overcome the bitterness and anger. In those writings, she saw a side of students she had never seen. I believe she could feel their pain in some cases, and clearly identify what they needed—love and compassion.

In the previous chapter, we discussed the power of mental association and explained how humans tend to link individuals with experiences.Cassandra's mental associations of those students were all negative until she read their letters. I believe the students outpouring of love and compassion enabled her to form a positive mental association. She saw them not only as youths who had bullied her son but as classmates who were in need of forgiveness. I'm convinced she became willing to overcome her own hurt and invade their personal space to reach out and comfort them.

Build Positive Mental Associations

Cassandra and I discovered the power of positive mental association and this important revelation can help you move to the next level. Unfortunately, you cannot remove the negative mental associations from your mind, but you can build positive associations if you're willing to interact with people who hurt you.

Can you relate to what Cassandra and I went through? Are there isolated and abandoned relationships in your life? Does the very presence of a person make you feel uncomfortable, angry, or even depressed? Do you shy away from phone calls and other attempts of contact by certain people?

If your answer is yes, you can start your evaluation by examining your mental associations with those individuals. What mental thoughts, memories, or emotions come to mind when you hear that person's name? Is it shame, anger, or abandonment? Does the act of what that person said or did lodge itself in your mind and create a flood of painful emotions?

Here is a word of wisdom: You feel what you focus on. Excessive thinking about the bad can lead to negative fixation that can usher in negative emotions of fear, anxiety, and anger. But if you focus on good and positive experiences, odds are positive emotions of peace, joy, and happiness will come. Do you have any positive mental associations with that person? Perhaps the relationship was good at some point. If so, I encourage you to focus on the good.

However, it's difficult to force the mind to think certain thoughts. Therefore, I want to share three tips to assist with what I call mental transformation.

Step One: Repeat positive things.

Say them out loud—allowing the ears to hear as well as the mouth to speak. Some refer to this practice as positive reinforcement. Notice there is no emphasis on addressing the negative because the purpose is to bring the positive to the forefront of the mind. While I do not recommend denying the bad, I believe focusing on it will not lead to peace within nor relationship reconciliation.

Years ago, I had a conversation with a friend about a difficult divorce he and his spouse of many years were going through. After several minutes of negative, but truthful statements about his wife, I asked him if anything good came from their years of marriage. He paused for a few seconds, and answered, "Our two children."

I asked him that question for a reason. I wanted him to focus on some good of the relationship and not be overcome by the bad.

Step Two: Meditate on the good.

Step one involved the mouth and ears. This step involves making a mental imprint on the mind through constant mental repetition until the thought becomes second nature. This can be accomplished through reading and rereading, writing and rewriting, and engaging in moments of meditation.

Write down a list of good things the person said or did. Read that list, slowly, at least once per day. Meditate on that list until you can recall it with little to no problem. Make a pact with yourself that if or when you see that person you will stop all activity and recall that list at least once.

If you do this successfully, I believe your mental battle will be conquered. For some it may take days, weeks, or even months, but in the end, all the hard work will pay off.

Step three: Interact with the person.

This could be, depending on the offense, the most difficult step to accomplish. As mentioned in pervious chapters, care and wisdom should be taken when interacting with individuals under certain circumstances. Be wise who you interact with and how it takes place but be passionate in your pursuit of relationships that should be restored.

As a human, you can tend to naturally avoid hurtful situations and often refuse to deal with the shame and disappointments of past relationships, instead resorting to living with the extended distance between yourself and others. You can avoid fighting through the unpleasant encounters to restore a peaceful and productive fellowship. Without a doubt, hurtful confrontations are hard to face and overcome.

But this is where God the Father sets the supreme example. He consistently pursues His creation despite the hurt we bring upon Him. Yes, the Lord does have feelings. He, too, can feel rejected, unloved, and ignored. Yet He loves us, and instead of settling for permanent separation, He pursues us through multiple avenues. He wants to restore a good relationship. He never stops loving and wanting us.

What about you? Is the broken relationship between you and your sibling, parent, or former spouse worth restoring? Have you simply accepted the icy barrier and convinced yourself it is for the best? Will you build up the courage to rise to the last level of forgiveness and pursue the person as God pursues you?

God's Pursuit

There are many examples in the Bible that demonstrate God's pursuit and His tireless effort to win over or win back people to Himself. In other words, He lives and operates on level three forgiveness. His only Son, Jesus Christ, walks on the same level of forgiveness.

God the Father invites a disobedient people to humble

themselves, pray, and turn from their wicked ways in order to experience the joy and peace of a good relationship.

"If My people who are called by My name will humble themselves, and pray and seek My face, and turn from their wicked ways, then I will hear from heaven, and will forgive their sin and heal their land."(2 Chronicles 7:14)

Jesus demonstrates level three forgiveness by interacting with Peter (Simon) face-to-face. Peter was one of His closest disciples but denied Jesus three times. After Jesus was raised from the dead, He restored the relationship between Peter and Himself by asking a series of questions:

He said to him the third time, "Simon, son of Jonah,[c] do you love Me?" Peter was grieved because He said to him the third time, "Do you love Me?" And he said to Him, "Lord, You know all things; You know that I love You." Jesus said to him, "Feed My sheep."(John 21:17)

Like Jesus pursued Peter in the preceding scripture, If you never seek to interact with the person who hurt you, opportunities to build positive associations may never occur.

If that happens, how will that unresolved issue affect you? I encourage and in some ways plead with you to make the decision to walk on level three forgiveness and interact with that person to correct and restore the relationship.

God's Love

The Christian Bible is a love story. It describes the incredible passion and compassion the Lord has for mankind. At points during the story, the relationship between them is clearly broken, fragile, and even destroyed during times of extreme sin by mankind. However, the Lord demonstrates mercy and grace—refusing to totally destroy them.

There is a message in this reoccurring theme: man's violations followed by God's forgiveness, redemption, and restoration. The Lord blesses mankind. They are obedient for a short time but eventually stray. He warns, punishes, and separates Himself from them. But almost always, He eventually extends an olive branch of hope to them. When humans truly repent and seek a return to the ways that please the Lord, He accepts their apology, forgives, and heals them.

The culmination of how God seeks to repair relationships is found in the New Testament. The creator of the universe and lover of people placed Himself in a human body (Jesus Christ), took the punishment meant for disobedient man (death on a cross), and raised Himself from the dead in order to draw all people to Himself. Christianity is all about a restored and revived relationship between the creator and the created (man).

The Lord of creation is a passionate pursuer. For His creation, He descends into the deepest valleys (heartaches) of their lives to comfort and encourage. He ascends the highest mountains (successes) of their experiences to share in their joy and happiness. He crosses the widest seas (obstacles) in their daily struggles to reassure and encourage them. This demonstrates His great love for them. No matter what they've done, no matter where they are in life, He wants to be close to them.

You and I can learn something from God's passionate love

and pursuit. What is His focus? He focuses on His love for us, not the many things we've done wrong. You and I were created for good acts of kindness and compassion, even though we often do the opposite. Our loving heavenly Father constantly separates our bad actions from who we really are and focuses on our potential.

Do you see the pattern, and can you apply this to your thinking? If you adopt God's view of seeing a person for who he or she could be as opposed to what he or she did, what impact would that make in your life? Would you passionately pursue that person as God pursues you? Would you forgive with perfect forgiveness (from the heart), reach out to the person, and act in love as you seek to restore or build a healthy relationship? Would you see as the Lord sees and realize people are not what they've done.

The person who raped or molested you has greater in him. The close friend whom you trusted with everything should not be equated to his or her act of betrayal. The person who senselessly murdered your loved one committed a horrible act that turned your life upside down, but even that person was created for greater by God.

Thus, the Lord continues His pursuit, even of those who have carried out horrific acts because He's calling to the good in them. Can you do the same?

Can you see the pattern, motivation, and focus? That should also be your motivation in reconciliation—to bring out the decency in others.

You may think, *I can't be like that and I can't just let things go*. Do you mean you can't or you won't? You can do whatever you desire to do if you want it badly enough. Do you want it?

The Need for God

True forgiveness cannot be achieved without having God in your life who provides all the necessary components to overcome the challenges of forgiveness.

- He provides the knowledge that leads to a higher level of thinking. (Isaiah 55:8-10)

- He provides the peace that surpasses all human understanding. (Isaiah 26:3)

- He gives the needed strength to carry out the difficult acts of kindness. (2 Corinthians 12:8-10)

- He gives true joy in those days and hours that seem to take their mental toll. (Isaiah 61:1-3)

- He calms the anger before it progresses to the point of no return. (1 Corinthians 10:13)

- God gives that one ray of hope when all else seems hopeless. (Romans 15:13-14)

Perfect forgiveness will involve all of you—body, soul, mind, and spirit. The Bible declares God is Spirit. Some refer to the spirit realm as supernatural. I've shared in this chapter that God and Jesus Christ both walk on level three forgiveness. If you also wish to operate on the highest level, you will need supernatural assistance from God.

Human intellect, talent, or desire alone cannot lead to perfect forgiveness. The pinnacle level of forgiveness is a type of divine forgiveness that surpasses human understanding and ability. The human mind, in regards to forgiveness, must be transformed into the mind of Christ. Human desires for revenge and condemnation must be converted to desires of mercy and restoration. The human will must be altered from self-gratification to seeking the good of the offender. All of these operations are done by the Spirit of God by the awesome power of God. Perfect forgiveness is beyond human capability.

How do we get this much-needed divine makeover? By accepting Jesus Christ as our Lord and Savior. When we accept Jesus Christ, we come into agreement with God and the Scriptures that proclaim God was in Jesus, reconciling Himself unto the world. We accept the fact that Jesus Christ died for our sins and that God raised Him from the dead. And we agree to live our lives according to the Word of God and the will of God.

I know from experience. If I faced the heartaches in my life without Jesus Christ and a personal relationship with God the Father, I would certainly be lost in depression. I'm not talking about becoming religious or joining a denomination. I'm talking about forming a real relationship with a living person who loves and cares for you.

Through this relationship, God makes His presence known in multiple ways. His presence revolves around His desires for me and my need for Him. In my loneliness, He gives me comfort and reassurance of His love for me.

When I'm feeling overcome with anger or anxiety, He comes to me and blankets me with His peace. When I need to talk to someone, He is there waiting to listen and speak words of encouragement into my heart. But most of all, He alone understands me better than I understand myself. He knows my mistakes, shortcomings, and ungodly desires, yet wants to form a solid relationship with me. He helps, coaches, and disciplines me through the tough times of my life.

God is a personal God. He forms relationships and has expectations for all those who receive Him. He is not some mystical figment of someone's imagination. He is very real and active in the lives of those who accept Him. God wants to do the same for anyone who believes He exists and accepts Jesus Christ as his or her Savior. God doesn't require background checks, applications, or references. He does not insist that you or I be perfect before giving our lives to Him. He just wants us to come to Him—just the way we are—right now.

If this sounds like someone you need in your life, I suggest you pray these words:

"Heavenly Father, I need you to help me through these hard times. I believe you are the creator of all, and I believe Jesus Christ is your only Son, sent to save me from my sins. I accept Jesus Christ as my Lord and Savior, and I give my life totally to you. Fill me with your holy presence and help me walk in perfect forgiveness. In Jesus' name, amen."

If you prayed that prayer and were sincere in your heart, Jesus Christ just saved you and wrote your name in the Book of Life in heaven. Now, rejoice in God's mercy and grace but also seek out a good Christian church that you can join.

Self-Examination: Level Three Forgiveness

Where is My Focus?

My focus is where God's focus is: upon restoration. I have matured in my thinking and now see things as the Lord does. I want to carry out His will, please Him, and reach out to someone in need.

How do I see the offender?

I finally realize that my hurt isn't totally about me. It's about the need of another. I see the person who hurt me as a person in need of loving correction, and I'm willing to become a party to that assignment.

How is My Relationship with God?

I'm closer to God and can sense His peace. I have stopped trailing the Lord and am now walking beside Him in terms of desire, passion, and forgiveness.

What's controlling me?

The controlling factor is my love for God and love for the person who hurt me. I realize love always seeks to repair, reclaim, and restore while hatred seeks to separate, destroy, and condemn. I choose to walk in love.

How do I move to the next level?

I've made it to the highest level of forgiveness. But I must be careful not to fall from this level. I will continue to keep my eyes on God and focus on the needs of the individual.

CHAPTER

6

ADOPTING THE POSTURE AND PRINCIPLES

I want to share something with you that I refer to as the posture of forgiveness. It is not a physical stance but a mental, emotional, and spiritual state of mind achieved by a daily commitment to forgive at a moment's notice. This posture involves the following.

- An Open Mind

  I declare that I am not above Jesus. If people hurt Him, they will hurt me. I have an open mind and realize people will hurt, hate, and sin against me. I refuse to build a fence around myself in an attempt to prevent the hurt. When the hurt comes, I will give them the benefit of the doubt, and I will forgive.

  Do you consider yourself too faithful to be betrayed?

Are you too good to be hated? Are you too committed to be left behind? If so, you may have the wrong view about yourself and life in general. In the real world, you and I are not shielded from the dark intentions of others. Therefore, we should not become overwhelmed with astonishment when bad things happen to us at the hands of people we know and love.

(John 15:18-21, John 16:33, 1Peter 2:23)

- Open Eyes

  I see people as my heavenly Father sees them, hurting and in need of healing. Therefore my desire is not for revenge but for them to be saved and come into the knowledge of the truth.

  Can you see past your pain and into the need of your perpetrator? Do you think something was missing in that person's life? If so, what do you think it was? Why do you think he or she hurt you?

  While it may be impossible for you to know what's in another person's mind or even their intentions, it is also important to evaluate your thoughts concerning him or her. Have you harshly assumed the bad and condemned him or her without proof?

  (1 Timothy 2:3-4, Isaiah 1:18, John 3:16)

- Open Mouth

  I am prepared to speak the words of forgiveness. I will open my mouth and say, *I forgive you.*My emotions may not want me to say it, but I am not controlled by my emotions. I am controlled by the word and will of God.

Are you willing to release words of freedom even though it may be the most difficult thing you've ever done? Will you follow what's right and just, or will you succumb to the damaging emotions of anger and bitterness?

(Proverbs 12:18, Proverbs 18:21, Luke 23:34)

• An Open Heart

I give others room to hurt me.I realize no one is perfect and that all have sinned and fallen short of the glory of God. I will not hold anyone to a standard they cannot achieve. I open my heart to forgive at a moment's notice.

Do you acknowledge that the people in your life aren't perfect? Will you give them space to disappoint and sin against you? Will you allow them to be human without expecting a pain-free relationship?

(Matthew 15:18, Matthew 18:34-35, Romans 3:23, 1 John 1:18)

• Open Arms

I stand ready to embrace anyone and receive him or her back into my life. I will not separate myself from anyone unless there is a good reason. I stand ready to love, bless, and do good to anyone who hurts me.

Will you give that person another chance to be close to you? Can you place him or her back on your good list and remove him or her from your blackball list? Does that person know he or she is welcomed to be by your side and to share in your life again?

(1 Corinthians 16:23, 1 Peter 4:8-10, James 3:17)

Notice all the positions indicate a willingness to be open,which means being vulnerable, but not unwise, with others. Trusting some people with our most guarded and prized secrets, thoughts, and experiences can be a very difficult thing to do. But the alternative is a closed mind, heart, eyes, arms, and mouth, all of which tend to isolate and separate. Being closed will not stop hurt from coming. It just makes it more difficult to deal with.

Are you an open person? Do you have an open mind? Are your eyes open? Do you have an open mouth ready to grant forgiveness? Do you have an open heart? Do you have open arms ready to invite someone back into your life?

Being open does not mean being careless or unwise in how we interact with others. Instead, it means you and I are aware of the possibilities of hurt and disappointments, but we have positioned ourselves to forgive at a moment's notice.

Principles of Forgiveness

I want to share several principles to practice while asking for and granting forgiveness. Some are harder to practice than others, but if you continue to work at them,you will eventually master them. I advise you to keep at it until them become second nature. Even if you fail at some, repent and try again until you get it right.

When Asking Others to Forgive You

Address your actions only, not those of the other person. When you've done wrong, keep the focus on your actions and do not attempt to justify your mistakes by blaming it on another.

Wrong: "I'm sorry for saying those mean things to you, but you should not have lied to me."

Right: "I'm sorry for saying those mean things to you. I am your friend and friends should be there for each other. Can you forgive me?"

Go beyond saying I'm sorry and say what you did. This shows you understand the details of the wrong and have given it sufficient thought.

Wrong: "I'm sorry for what I said. So now can we get some dinner on the table?"

Right: "I'm sorry for disrespecting you, especially in front of others. A husband should love his wife, not humiliate her. Can you forgive me?"

Show sincerity in your tone and posture. Your voice and body language are indicators of true feelings and motives. Things such as avoiding eye contact or folding of the arms are signs of insincerity. Give the person your full attention, make eye contact, and speak softly. A kind jester may include a touch on the shoulder or hand depending on the closeness of the relationship.

When Others Ask You for Forgiveness

Accept the person's apology right away and forgive. Say the

words, "I forgive you, and I accept your apology," regardless of how you feel at the moment." Remember, forgiving is not tied to emotions. You can and should forgive, even while angry or hurt. My advice is to grant forgiveness and deal with the emotions later.

Avoid sharing what the person did to you with those who don't have a need to know. In the Christian faith, spreading unneeded negative information about another is called gossip and can do more damage to relationships than the actual offense. You should not further damage a person's reputation if possible. Love covers certain wrongs. Love is evidence of maturity.

Avoid bringing up the matter with the person, especially during disagreements. When you have forgiven someone, let their past acts go and do not remind the person of what he or she did. True forgiveness releases the person from the act. Constantly rehashing a matter is proof you have not forgiven from the heart.

If you have asked for forgiveness or forgiven others in the past, did your actions line up with all these principles? Perfecting them will take time, so do not become disheartened if you fail at some of them at certain times. Repent and try again until you master them.

CHAPTER

7

FORGIVING PERSECUTION

At the writing of this book, rogue groups formed in several countries with the sole purpose of carrying out atrocities against men, women, and children. Refugee camps swelled to near impossible numbers to accommodate and in themselves, are places of danger for the unprotected. Some of the most disturbing acts of persecution have taken place on the continent of Africa and in select areas of the Middle East.

It is common to see disturbing media images of innocent people fleeing wars, terrorism, and famine, often carrying helpless children in their arms.

In persecution, it is common for individuals to be imprisoned, tortured, or maimed for life. Accounts of unspeakable violence and dehumanization have been reported by several human rights groups. Victim and eye witness accounts of gruesome acts against women and children, in particular females, often include brutal rape and defacing which leaves victims with a physical reminder of the incident.

In the reality of such horrific encounters, how can a person forgive something that has scarred them, seemingly for life?

If you have experienced persecution or know someone who has, do you think it's possible to walk on level three forgiveness toward someone who has committed such acts? The process of forgiving may be much harder due to the depth of physical, mental, and emotional pain—but it is possible.

According to the Christian faith, there is no limit to what should be forgiven. No matter how hurtful or humiliating the offense, the Lord Jesus Christ instructs and expects His followers to forgive. But because He knows our deepest fears and pains, He is willing to be patient and give supernatural assistance during the long and challenging journey to forgive.

I want to share some keys to forgiving persecution. If you have been persecuted, I ask you to take it to heart. If you know someone who has, please share these keys with that person.

Key 1: Identify the real enemy.

It is natural to view the attacker as the enemy. After all, it was this person who carried out those awful acts. But I urge a deeper look under the covers of persecution to see who is really behind it all.

In Revelation 2:10, Jesus Christ sent a message to the people of the church at Smyrna to warn them about the persecution that is about to come upon them.

> "Do not fear any of those things which you are about to suffer. Indeed, the devil is about to throw some of you into prison, that you may be tested, and you will have tribulation ten days. Be faithful until death, and I will give you the crown of life."

Notice in these Scriptures that Jesus identifies the persecutor as the devil, not the people. This is the one the Bible calls Satan— the accuser of mankind. He is a real fallen spirit who is active in the world and among people. His primary job is to kill, steal, and destroy. He does this by taking advantage of a person's evil desires or lack of knowledge. At times he makes suggestions, plants thoughts, and stirs up emotions of anger, hatred, and jealously.

Yet the devil cannot force people to commit persecution. Ultimately, they do it because they have chosen to. Thus, individuals, through their own lust and desires, often become participants used and influenced by the devil to carry out demeaning acts of violence.

Persecutors need to be delivered from the unholy influence of the devil. They need Jesus Christ. They need a miraculous transformation of desire, heart, and mind. The only way to get that divine transformation is by being saved and filled with the Holy Spirit of God. Therefore, you must realize the identity of the real enemy: the devil.

Key 2: Forgive your persecutor.

It has been said that the best revenge is forgiveness. I've written
several chapters in this book on steps to forgive, but nowhere have
I suggested or implied that forgiving is easy. In fact, depending on
the depth of hurt, forgiving can be extremely difficult. However,
forgiveness is preferred because it brings with it peace and joy.

If you decide to follow the process and steps outlined in this
book, your burden of anger and hatred will be removed, even
though it may take months or years. Do you want to experience
the true freedom of forgiveness?

Key 3: Share the gospel with your persecutor.

When saved, the person receives a new nature—a desire to do
good and please the Lord. The old evil desires are still present,
but the Holy Spirit of God is constantly at work in that person's
life, convicting him or her about the bad and urging him or her to
do good.

Therefore, the best way to respond to persecution is to introduce
the persecutor to Jesus Christ. In the following Scriptures, the
Christians Paul and Silas were falsely accused, brutally beaten,
and thrown into prison to await their death sentence.

"And when they had laid many stripes on them, they threw them into
prison, commanding the jailer to keep them securely. Having received
such a charge, he put them into the inner prison and fastened their feet
in the stocks.

But at midnight Paul and Silas were praying and singing hymns to

God, and the prisoners were listening to them. Suddenly there was a great earthquake, so that the foundations of the prison were shaken; and immediately all the doors were opened and everyone's chains were loosed.

And the keeper of the prison, awaking from sleep and seeing the prison doors open, supposing the prisoners had fled, drew his sword and was about to kill himself. But Paul called with a loud voice, saying, "Do yourself no harm, for we are all here."

Then he called for a light, ran in, and fell down trembling before Paul and Silas. And he brought them out and said, "Sirs, what must I do to be saved?"

So they said, "Believe on the Lord Jesus Christ, and you will be saved, you and your household." Then they spoke the word of the Lord to him and to all who were in his house. And he took them the same hour of the night and washed their stripes. And immediately he and all his family were baptized. Now when he had brought them into his house, he set food before them; and he rejoiced, having believed in God with all his household."(Acts 16:23-34)

Paul and Silas must have forgiven the jailer. Immediately after the earthquake, the jailor thought the prisoners had escaped and drew his sword to commit suicide. But Paul and Silas called to him and stopped him from hurting himself. It is obvious they did not wish any harm to come to the jailor.

I believe Paul and Silas walked on level three forgiveness toward the jailer. Can you do the same toward your persecutors?

Are you saved? Do you have a testimony about what Jesus Christ means to you, and can you share that good news with someone who tormented you?

Perhaps the gospel may be just the thing your persecutor needs. Can you be the person who shares it in a safe way—perhaps through a letter or other means of communication. Do you think hearing the gospel would change your persecutor?

CHAPTER

8

FORGIVING YOURSELF

I had a very difficult time forgiving myself after my son's death. The tremendous guilt for not spending enough time with him and the shame for not being the father he deserved took their emotional toll. Days after his burial, thoughts of regret flooded my mind and depression gripped my soul.

How could I have allowed precious time to pass so quickly and missed so many precious moments with him? I knew better. I understood the importance of a balanced life, but I failed to live what I knew.

How can I make it up to him? How can I turn back the hands of time and redo our relationship? How do I remove this tremendous burden of guilt that feels like a three-hundred-pound gorilla? How do I forgive myself? These questions dominated my thought process for weeks.

Maybe your situation was more serious than a guilty conscience. Was it an accident that you wish with all your heart could be undone? Was it something done or said, without much thought, that caused a tremendous strain in a valuable relationship? Was it a missed opportunity to tell someone how much he or she meant to you before it was too late. Did you make a bad decision that led to the loss of life? Have you forgiven yourself?

At times, it may be easier to forgive others than ourselves. Yet the same process used to forgive others should be used for self-forgiveness. One possible reason for the struggle is what I refer to as dual-role forgiveness.

The first role is that of the asker—a person who asks another, "Would you please forgive me?"

The second role is that of granter. This person grants forgiveness by saying, "I accept your apology, and I forgive you."

In self-forgiveness, one person must walk in both roles. He or she must acknowledge his or her fault in the incident, apologize, and ask for forgiveness. Then, he or she must grant forgiveness to himself or herself by saying, "I forgive you," or in this case, "I forgive me."

In dual-role forgiveness, the same principles discussed in earlier chapters apply. We should ask and answer the same questions:

Why should I ask for forgiveness?

Because I want to acknowledge my wrong and make things right with another—in this case, with myself.

Why should I grant forgiveness?

Because I want to extend mercy and grace and enjoy a peaceful relationship with myself.

You may ask, how do I ask for forgiveness and receive it at the same time? Here is an example.

Carolyn's years of drug abuse tore her family apart—even leading to the abandonment of her two children and a bitter divorce from her childhood sweetheart. Now, after several years of successful drug treatment, she was finally ready to face the family she brought so much pain upon. She laid full blame at her own feet and often drowned in the guilt of her babies growing up without their mother. Before she approached them to ask for forgiveness, she needed to first forgive herself. She stood in front of a mirror.

"Carolyn," she said, "I am so sorrow for all the pain and disappointment I brought into your life. I made the wrong choices for the wrong reasons and hurt you in many ways. Can you please forgive me?"

She closed her eyes, took a deep breath, and imagined herself as the other person.

"Carolyn," she said, "yes, those years of pain hurt, but I never stopped loving you. I accept your apology, and I forgive you from my heart."

She put her arms around herself and gently squeezed. Tears flowed as she received her own forgiveness, love, and acceptance. Finally, she could begin a new life—one without guilt, shame, and depression. She felt like a new person, and in a sense, she was.

THE NEXT LEVEL FORGIVER

Your process of self-forgiveness does not have to happen in the same manner, but it does need to occur in a way that's comfortable to you.

If you're struggling to forgive yourself, at some point, you should acknowledge your part, apologize, and ask for forgiveness. You should also grant forgiveness to yourself. It is the only way to find peace.

True Versus False Guilt

Guilt, in certain situations, can be a good thing. It is a sign that you and I have an active and sensitive conscience. When we do the wrong things, especially things that hurt others, we should experience guilt. But that feeling doesn't have to drive us into depression. It lets us know we need to make amends as best we can.

On the other hand, there is something called false guilt—which is blaming ourselves for something we had no control over or did not know.

For example, a person who was raped may experience false guilt and blame herself by constantly questioning her actions, dress, or words. She may ask these questions:

Did I do or say something to mislead the person?

Were my clothes too revealing?

Why did I allow myself to be alone with that person?

In this situation, these questions reveal a sense of false guilt. While there may be lessons to learn, she was in no way responsible for the rape. In the end, the rapist had control over himself and never should have forced himself on her. She is not responsible for his actions.

Are you dealing with a situation of false guilt? Are you blaming yourself for another person's choice or for something you had no control over? If so, it's time to release the false guilt and usher peace into your life. Please repeat the following statements.

I put away the false guilt for what happened.

It was not my fault nor my responsibility.

I did not cause it and was not aware of what would happen.

I release myself from false guilt and invite peace into my life.

A suggested prayer:

Heavenly Father, please help me let go of false guilt and usher peace into my mind and emotions. Reassure me of your love and acceptance and fill me with your holy presence. In the name of Jesus Christ, I pray. Amen.

CHAPTER

9

RECOGNIZING THE ENEMIES OF FORGIVENESS

In the Bible, the Apostle Paul shared the human dilemma with doing right. I will paraphrase his words found in Romans 7:21.

Deep down inside, we all want to do the right thing, but instead, we end up doing the wrong thing.

He explained something always stood in the way of carrying out good deeds. That something was sin—the temptation and the urge to commit wrong. He implied sin was the enemy of righteousness and godliness. His solution was the a relationship with Jesus Christ, the Son of the living God.

This is also true when it comes to forgiving others. There

are enemies at work in your life and in mine, both within us and external to us, that fight against our desires to do carry out godly deeds. I want to share a few of those enemies.

As you read about them, please take a moment to reflect on your personal situation. Determine if a particular enemy is alive and active in your life. Ask and answer the tough questions:

Is this the enemy holding me back?

Is this why forgiving is so hard for me?

How do I conquer this and move to the next level?

Enemy 1: Ungodly Pride

In the Bible, Jesus shared a story about a man whose ungodly pride prevented him from forgiving a person who owed him money. Needless to say, the story did not end well for the prideful man. His elevated ego landed him in prison among the tormentors.

Ungodly pride can be defined as a lofty sense of self-importance. Here are a few common thoughts and misconceptions that may indicate the presence of pride.

1. I believe my refusal to forgive is hurting my abuser.

2. I can't believe you did that to me! I deserve better!

3. I don't have to take this, and I won't!

4. I'll always hold this against you, and I'll never forgive!

5. I refuse to forgive because…

Do any of these thoughts, words, or misconceptions sound familiar? Notice the constant emphasis on self often found in the words **I**, **me**, and **my**.

I'm too important!

This shouldn't happen to me!

You need to beg for my forgiveness!

I have a good reason not to forgive you!

None of us is above hurt, abuse, or betrayal. We all are subject to the pain and disappointment from life and relationships. I want to share a grim reality:

There are some people who don't like you, and it doesn't have to be for any particular reason.

Not everyone is supportive of you or your endeavors. Some people in your life will seem committed but really aren't, and their lack of commitment will expose itself in time.

My point in saying these things is to drive home the facts. Life isn't all good. But thankfully, life isn't all bad either. So we must deal with the good and the bad.

If you have contemplated, said, or adopted any of these signs of pride, I implore you to confess it, seek forgiveness from God, and work to become free from its deadly grip.

Is ungodly pride your enemy?

Enemy 2: Spiritual Immaturity

Jesus referred to two of his closest followers as sons of thunder. This nickname wasn't a compliment. It was a stinging criticism of their lack of spiritual maturity.

The two had been rejected while witnessing in the streets and afterward, wanted to call down fire and destroy those who refused their testimonies. Because of their lack of maturity, they wanted to return hurt for hurt.

Jesus quickly and firmly rebuked them, noting that they did not realize the purpose nor importance of the power they had been given. He implied their assignment was to save, build, and heal, not to damn, destroy, and tear down. Their mission was to help others, regardless of how they were treated.

For most people, it's very difficult to return good for bad. Deep within lies the desire to treat others as we have been treated instead of treating others as we want to be treated.

Often, we are tempted to make others feel the same pain, experience the same trauma, and carry the same heavyburden that was strapped to our shoulders.

This desire is the result of a lack of spiritual maturity. The answer is growth—both in knowledge and in spirituality. The Christian faith calls this *transformation*—viewing things from the mind of God and not from our human minds. It involves learning God's viewpoint on the situation and meditating on it until His way becomes our way.

Then, our thought process and desires will begin to change and line up with the mind of God. Transformation is the process of changing into the mature person our heavenly Father wants us to become. He wants us to focus on healing others even when we have been hurt by them. Here are a few biblical Scriptures that indicate His will.

"You have heard that it was said, 'You shall love your neighbor and hate your enemy.' But I say to you, love your enemies, bless those who curse you, do good to those who hate you, and pray for those who spitefully use you and persecute you, that you may be sons of your Father in heaven; for He makes His sun rise on the evil and on the good, and sends rain on the just and on the unjust. ..."(Matthew 5:43-48)

"Repay no one evil for evil. Have regard for good things in the sight of all men." (Romans 12:17)

"Do not be overcome by evil, but overcome evil with good." (Romans 12:21)

What's your desire? Do you want to hurt or heal? Could spiritual immaturity be your enemy?

Enemy 3: Unconfessed and Unexpressed Hurt

"I've never talked about it, and I've never told anyone. It's something hidden in my past, and I want it keep it buried."

As a biblical counselor, I've heard similar statements from people during private discussions. The thought that immediately surfaces in my mind is *it may be buried, but it's not dead.*

Unconfessed and unexpressed issues that have been buried alive have a tendency to resurrect with even more power than they had prior to the funeral. In other words, the failure to properly address hurtful occurrences only leads to deeper pain and can trigger the onset of emotional instability, mental problems, and even physical illness.

After the death of my son, I struggled with several things but hid them from my wife, family, and friends in the clergy. I covered the guilt, shame, anger, and doubting of my faith. But then I discovered my love for writing and began to express my struggles using a pen and paper.

Through books, I exposed and conquered those areas of my life. Now, I can honestly say I've become better instead of bitter.

Have you conquered or covered the tragedies and disappointments in your life? Here are some signs of covering:

1. Refusal to discuss it with anyone.

2. The hurt and pain is still fresh after a long time.

3. It has made you bitter, distrustful, and prejudiced toward anyone who resembles or reminds you of the person who hurt you.

In contrast, here are some signs of conquering:

1. You no longer wish ill on the person who hurt you. It's okay to want justice, but not revenge.

2. You have shared it, in a constructive manner, with a faithful person you can trust.

3. You can talk about it if led and share a positive testimony about your growth.

Can you see the difference between covering and conquering? Where are you? Have you covered, or conquered?

You cannot conquer what you refuse to face. Yes, facing it will hurt. The painful emotions and recollections will return, but if you confront them and seek professional or spiritual assistance, you can overcome all the negativity of the circumstance. Perhaps not overnight, in a week, or even in a few months. But I believe you will, eventually, win the battle.

Could unexpressed or unconfessed hurt be your issue?

CHAPTER

10

WHAT NOW? WALK ME THROUGH IT

The healing begins with you. If you're not walking on the top level of forgiveness, there is work ahead. First make up your mind and commit to change. Do you see the value in forgiving and releasing the tremendous burden of hatred and anger?

The first step is mental—determining within yourself that things have to and will change for the better. You must reach the conclusion that a lack of change would be far worse than the challenging road to change. Can you visualize the end goal? You will have more peace, joy, and happiness, not only within yourself but among your family and friends.

The second step is to determine what level you are on and decide on a course of action that will lead to the next level. Are you on level zero? If so, you need to discover which enemy of forgiveness is holding you back, and take the necessary steps to conquer and climb to level one.

If you're on level one, you need to work on how you perceive your enemy. Are you unjustly separating yourself? If so, why? What will it take to overcome the wall of separation and walk up the steps to reconciliation? Are you ready to do more than the basics?

If you're on level two, prayer for the person who hurt you is the right thing to do. But is it all the Lord wants you to do? Is there some small part God is calling you to carry out, perhaps to demonstrate true love?

If you're on the top level, level three, where you are interacting with the person, showing him or her the love of God, I celebrate with you. But your work may not be complete until the person recognizes his or her faults and seeks to make amends. In other words, continue demonstrating God's grace. It may take some people time to respond to kindness.

Here is a story that demonstrates the importance of taking the first step.

Example: Jeneva rang the doorbell to her father's house, but she didn't want to. As she stood on the porch nervously waiting for the elderly man to answer the door, her mind faded back to those moments of abuse he inflicted on her as a child.

Those wounds of abuse had managed to destroy her twelve-year marriage and separate her from her children. Now, two years after a divorce and release from a mental institution, she was finally preparing to confront the man whom she often said "destroyed my life."

But during the past two years, Jeneva managed to find Christ in an intimate way. It was because of His healing, comforting, and strengthening that she was able to bring herself to her father's doorstep. Now, she was being led by the Holy Spirit to confront her abuser and she didn't have a clue what she would say or do.

As she prayerfully waited, the door slowly opened. She gazed upon the face of her father for the first time in over ten years.

"Hi," Jeneva said, as she forced a smile on her face.

He seemed surprised to see her and after a moment of staring, managed to mumble, "It's been a long time. I thought you forgot about me after your mother died."

Jeneva felt very awkward, and he finally motioned for her to come in. As they took their seats, the conversation turned to the usual small talk. He didn't seem to take much interest when she updated him on her failed marriage and family. In fact, he didn't seem surprised at all by the outcome of her life.

During a moment of silence, the Holy Spirit whispered to her, "Tell him you're sorry and ask him to forgive you."

What! Jeneva thought. Why should I do that? He was the one who abused me! After wrestling with the thought for several minutes she finally set her mind to do it.

She rose from her seat, "Well, I've got to go now, so maybe I will stop by some other time." She took a deep breath, knelt down in front of him, and took him by the hand.

"Dad, I know our relationship hasn't been like a real father and daughter, and I want you to know that I am sorry for not being there for you after mom passed away. I know I've never said this before, but I love you and I want you to love me, too. Please forgive me." Jeneva gave him a warm hug.

As they embraced, he burst into tears.

"What's wrong?" She asked.

All he could say was, "I'm sorry, sweetheart….I'm sorry…"

For the first time, he began to share the abuse from his childhood. As he spoke of those awful experiences, Jeneva held him tight, and they both continued to shed tears.

It was then the Holy Spirit helped her to understand something significant: Hurting people hurt others. Now she understood why the she was led to begin the healing. As they continued to embrace and cry together, God was at work, healing them both from years of hatred and abuse.

***

Can you identify with Jeneva? Are you being led to begin the healing? If so, I urge you to follow the lead.

CHAPTER

11

KNOWING IT'S NOT ABOUT YOU

"But you don't know how that made me feel! You don't understand!"

Those are words I hear frequently when discussing forgiveness in private sessions. The people who use them aren't bad people or mediocre Christians. They are God-loving individuals who have been deeply wounded by something or someone.

In my roundabout way, I always attempt to help them come to an important realization:

It's not about you.

You and I have the tendency to embrace and live by a self-centered view concerning troubles and trials. We can become so focused on ourselves that we miss the ultimate opportunity to reveal God to others as we go through difficult times.

We have opportunities to witness for God in suffering,

heartaches, and even in death. We all have what I call *platform moments* in our lives. I refer to them as platform moments because of what is written in the Word of God.

In 1 Corinthians 4:9, Paul writes about the worldly injustice the Apostles were experiencing. God had allowed his servants to be placed on a platform of suffering. Why? So the world could get a glimpse of God's glory.

I've been there. Done that. Got the t-shirt. I know what it's like to be on that platform.

A few days after my son passed away, I was preparing to deliver the eulogy at his funeral. Sitting there between my weeping wife and somber little daughter, I fixed my eyes on his casket a few feet away from us and suddenly discovered the pain was too great for me to bear.

After asking God for peace, I slowly stepped up to the pulpit. There was a moment of complete silence that seemed to last for hours. I believe many people in the audience were wondering about my walk with the Lord.

I wonder if He really knows Christ?

Is this Christian thing real?

Will he praise God or break down in tears?

I took a deep breath, glanced at our son's body, and began to speak.

You're probably wondering, why isn't he crying? I want you to know that I've been down in the valley. I've stumbled around in the darkness. I've had my moments when I've felt as weak as water. And I've cried till I have run out of tears.

But I also want you to know that my God has come. And He has strengthened me. He's picked up my feet out of the valley and placed them on the mountain top.

After those words, the people in that little church burst forth into praise. Some began to weep and others glorified God. I believe they realized my family was in the midst of the most hurtful moments of our lives, but God was with us. It wasn't about us. It was about Him!

I didn't realize it at the time, but I believe God allowed us to be placed on that platform. Thank God we used it to give Him glory. Even in one of the darkest times of our lives, we helped people see past our pain to catch a glimpse of an awesome God.

Here is another story to demonstrate platform moments.

Clarissa sat silently in the huge auditorium two hours before she was to speak to a crowd of about six thousand people. As she meditated on the words to be delivered from the Scriptures, suddenly and softly, a voice spoke to her.

"Clarissa, it's not about you. It's about Me."

Then Clarissa understood why God allowed all those horrible things to invade her life. The crowds of people she encouraged, inspired, and led to the Lord were the fruit of many years of heartache and pain.

She had always thought the incest and rape was all about her. She was convinced the breast cancer was strictly about her. And certainly, losing the fairy-tail husband to a younger woman was totally about her. Now, she saw and understood things from a different point of view. She saw things through the eyes of God.

She also saw the Scriptures from a different perspective. When she reread the story about the man born blind, she could actually see herself in the man. Her only question was:

"Lord, how could you allow this man to be born blind, to suffer for so long, just to reveal your glory?"

As she continued to meditate, the answer came.

"He has been given a passion to testify to my name, and he has received much more reward than you can ever imagine."

***

I think we all can identify with Clarissa to some respect. We often think the unfortunate experiences in our lives are all about us.

Why did this have to happen to me?

What am I going to do now?

I am so hurt by all of this!

How can I continue to live after this?

If you think the hurtful occurrences in your life are all about you, you are dead wrong. Those disappointments are but platforms and spotlights yielding opportunities to show the world how good, faithful, and loving God is, even in the pain!

You may be on your platform as you read this book. If so, I'll give you a little wisdom.

What you're going through is not about you. It's all about God. Yes, it's happening to you, but it's not about you. So tell someone about His goodness, His mercy, and His love. Use your platform to His glory.

Suggested prayer: My great and loving Father. I don't understand the things I need to, but I know, in spite of the things that have happened to me, you love me. Help me to see my situation through your eyes and your mind. Help me to give you glory and praise. Help my lips to sing of your love forever. In the name of Jesus Christ, I pray. Amen.

Now please begin your journey of forgiveness by working through the forgiveness work booklet *The Next Level Forgiver Work Booklet*. Hardback and e-book versions are available. Please see the ministry website for details at clholley.org.

CHAPTER

12

LEADING OTHERS TO FORGIVE

The goal of this book is to teach people how to forgive and to create a massive army of forgiveness leaders who are actively teaching and leading others.

In your everyday course of life, I'm convinced you will encounter many people who are struggling with, and perhaps sinking in, a sea of anger and hatred that often accompanies disappointments. They may be family members, close friends, coworkers, and even fellow church members.

What should you do? How can you recognize the need for forgiveness in the words and actions of others? Are you comfortable speaking with others about forgiveness? Do you know the words, methods, or techniques to use?

This chapter offers suggestions and techniques to use as you encourage others to forgive. These pointers are meant to be a starting point, not a complete set of instructions. Feel free to add techniques you feel safe using or to avoid those that make you nervous.

Recognizing the signs

- Anger or hatred

How does the person speak about another? Does he or she use words or phrases that demean, insult, or make another look bad? Here are some examples.

I don't like her, not one bit.

Yes, he walked out on me, but I don't care what he does.

I should have known not to trust her. I wish we'd never met.

He was never a father to me and will always be a no-good drunkard.

Hatred in words or actions toward or about another is a sign that person has not forgiven. Insults, slams, and constant put-downs of another's character often stem from a root of bitterness. It can be justified or unjustified and could be resident in the person for many years.

If you hear someone you know consistently casting a person in a negative light, it is an indicator the speaker has not forgiven. This may be a person with whom you need to share the good news of forgiveness.

- Avoidance of speaking about another

The refusal to address or discuss a person or hurtful situation could be an indicator of a lack of forgiveness. For some people, the pain may be too piercing to talk about.

During private counseling sessions, some clients say something similar to this:

"I can't bring that up without getting emotional, so I just don't talk about it."

My response is usually, "Does avoiding it help you heal and move forward with peace?"

The answer comes back as, "No, but I'm just not ready to face it."

I'm very sympathetic with him or her and choose not to push the issue beyond that question. I understand a person can't face it in a mature manner until he or she is ready to confront it.

If you encounter a person who is avoiding discussion of another person or unpleasant situation, please be wise and gather as much information as possible before deciding to address the issue.

Methods of Approach

- Indirect

You can talk to the person and speak to the situation without directly addressing his or her story. This can be done by sharing your personal testimony about forgiveness or by using a short story or lesson from a book or study.

I believe a personal testimony is most effective. People are usually interested in others who have gone through similar incidents and are inspired by people who have overcome. If you have an opportunity to share your story, do so with sincerity, truth, and conviction. Help that person to see and believe that if you overcame, they can also.

Example: Jake had worked with Steve for several years and the two became close after sharing their common life experiences with deadbeat dads. Although the details of their lives were different, both had to endure tough times without a father.

As they sat in the break room, Jake noticed Steve wasn't as talkative as usual.

"What's wrong man?" Jake asked.

"I can't believe that man is trying be a part of my life after all these years."

Jake responded, "That man?"

"You know, the one that shall remain nameless. He had the nerve to call my cellphone and leave a message to meet. I'm afraid of what I'll do if I set eyes on him."

Jake hesitated. "Oh, your dad."

"Not my dad," Steve snapped. "Just some man who threw our family away like yesterday's garbage."

Jake hung his head and smiled. "Steve, I know you've been hurt really bad. We've had similar experiences, so you know I can sympathize. But I want to share something that helped me overcome all the anger I had toward my dad."

Steve's face developed a curious expression.

Jake continued, "When my kids grew old enough to figure out they were missing a grandpa on my side, I thought long and hard about what they would miss out on if they never met him. I finally located and reached out to him to see if he had any interest in being in the lives of his grandchildren. And to my surprise, he did."

Steve interrupted, "That had to be tough on you."

Jake said, "I admit, the first several visits were very difficult and uncomfortable. But as I got to know him through his actions with my kids, I saw another side of the man I'd always hated. I've forgiven him for the hurtful rejection of the past, and I know my kids' lives are the better."

Steve seemed to take it all in as he stared at the break-room table. "I am tired of carrying the anger. Maybe I will give him a chance."

- Direct

When directly addressing the person's situation, please be careful not to offend or accuse the person. Take care to find words that are not confrontational or demeaning. Instead, gently point out the negative effects of the situation and encourage the person to address the issue in a constructive manner. Choose your words carefully. Words have power to break or build.

Example: Carol's best friend, Judy, was having a terrible day. As they walked through a department store, Judy appeared distant.

"Okay, Judy," Carol said, "I've known you too long not to know something's heavy on your mind. Out with it."

Judy flopped into a chair and threw her arms up in disgust. "I can't find anything I'm looking for!"

"Judy?" Carol said as she sat beside her. "What's wrong?"

Judy burst forth in tears as Carol immediately comforted her.

"It's my soon-to-be ex-husband. I know I'm not supposed to hate anyone, but I truly hate him."

"What's he done now?" Carol asked.

"He and his girlfriend have launched a lawsuit against me for full custody of our daughter. The lies listed on the suit are just outrageous. I can't believe I ever loved that sleezy con artist of a man!"

Carol embraced her best friend and allowed her to release pent-up frustration by weeping on Carol's shoulder.

"I'm so sorry, Judy," Carol said. "I had no idea he was capable of something so low. But my concern isn't for him. It's for you."

Judy glanced at Carol. "Me? Why are you concerned about me?"

"You haven't smiled in weeks," Carol said, "and you constantly have this distant look on your face. I can see you're not happy, and I believe your daughter notices it also."

Judy wiped her face and took a deep breath. "I can't pretend it's not happening."

"I know," Carol responded. "But you can forgive, release the anger and hatred, and embrace the peace it brings. I believe that's the best way to face this. Show him that you're not going to stoop to his level."

Judy glanced around the store. "I suppose you're right. I need your help with this one."

"You know I'm always here for you," Carol said as she hugged her best friend.

- Share

You can share material that addresses that person's situation and provides positive steps to bring healing, comfort, and peace. It can be a favorite book, electronic media, website or blog, or even a daily devotional. My advice is to follow up with the individual in a few days or weeks and to be patient. Give the person time and remember, different people have different time frames and preferences when it comes to healing.

Example: Elijah met Melanie at a youth church outing. The two became close over the following months, often spending time together on the phone and through social media.

Elijah noticed something strange about her whenever the subject turned to her mother. She routinely cut the conversation short by changing the subject. Finally, as they sat on the steps of the church after service, Elijah carefully brought up the issue.

"Melanie, I have something to ask you." Elijah said. "If you don't want to talk about it, you don't have it."

"What is it?" She asked.

"I notice every time I bring up your mom you avoid talking about her. In fact, I've haven't seen her with you and your dad. Is everything okay?"

Melanie lowered her head and sighed, but Elijah patiently waited for a reply.

"I don't talk about her because she is to blame for breaking up our family," she said. "She cheated on dad with a boy who could have been my older brother. When word got out, all of our lives were ruined. That's why dad and I moved here, to get a fresh start."

"Oh." Elijah said. "I'm sorry about that. I had no idea."

Melanie continued, "She tore down everything my dad worked so hard to build for us all, I don't think I can ever forgive her."

Elijah thought for a few seconds. "I can't begin to imagine how you feel, but I do know forgiveness is the best path to take. I have a really good book I believe will help. I can bring it, and you can keep it as long as you want and read whenever you feel up to it. Would you like me to bring it?"

"Yeah." Melanie said. "I don't know where to start but I do know I need to let go of all this hurt."

- *Refer*

    If you believe the person could benefit from personal contact with a professional or member of the clergy, you can provide a reference and follow up within a good time period. You can also accompany the person on they first visit to a counselor or confidant. But do so only if that person agrees with that type of assistance. Under no circumstances should you force it upon another. It must be his or her choice.

This option is often the choice for people who are experiencing a high degree of difficulty and whose life may become severely impacted if they do not receive help.

Example: The car line at middle school stretched around the corner of the building. Most parental drivers stood outside their vehicles on the warm day, engaging in chats. Sue and Catherine were regulars and often enjoyed interesting conversations.

"Hey, Sue," Catherine said. "I couldn't forget our last talk about our children. You mentioned some challenges with one in particular. Hope things worked out."

Sue frowned. "No. In fact, things have gone from bad to worse. And it's threatening my entire family. My husband and I disagree on how to handle it, and now we are having marital problems also."

"Oh, no," Catherine said. "I'm sorry to hear that."

"I don't know where to turn," Sue responded with a hint of desperation in her voice.

"I know a great counselor I've used to help me through a few things," Catherine said. She reached into her purse and pulled out the counselor's business card. "Give her a call and tell her I recommended you. I believe she can help all of you get through this."

Sue accepted the card and they embraced.

Summary

In your quest to help others, it may be necessary to use a combination of approaches to achieve the best success. It is not uncommon for some people to need a direct, indirect, and reference approach. You can determine which method to use and the best time to reach out.

The world is in need of forgiveness leaders. I pray you will incorporate these methods and approaches into your daily life as you walk among many people who have been hurt, rejected, and abused.

I encourage you to keep a journal of those you have talked to, shared with, or given references to. If possible, keep track of their progress, challenges, and successes. You may be surprised at how much your care and concern can affect the lives of others.

This concludes this book. I pray you have gleaned some things from it that will increase your level of forgiveness and help you reach out to others. May the Lord bless and keep you and your family.

About the Author

C.L. Holley was born in extreme poverty as the youngest of ten children, excelled to graduate from college and attained a Masters Degree. He overcame personal tragedy with the sudden death of his teenage son, advanced to found a powerful  ministry, and is the author of several inspirational books.

He was born in Alabama the son of a sharecropper and maid, the youngest of ten children. He spent his early years of 1960s growing up in a small neighborhood in Limestone county Alabama. Chopping cotton, picking strawberries, and raising farm animals was all he knew until he dared to dream big.

He is an ordained Minister, Author, and Speaker. He earned a B.S. in Business Administration and a Master of Biblical Counseling. He has a beautiful wife of over twenty-five years and is the father of two children—a beautiful daughter and a son who tragically died in 2001 at the age of thirteen. He loves to write books that encourage, inspire, and change the life of the reader for the better. With a powerful gift of communication and the ability to connect with the audience, he continues to speak soul-stirring inspiration to others and to write life changing books. He is a dynamic speaker who promotes his books nationally and internationally.

Visit CLHolley.org for more info.

FORGIVENESS JOURNAL

(This page has been left blank for your personal writings.)

FORGIVENESS JOURNAL

(This page has been left blank for your personal writings.)

FORGIVENESS JOURNAL

(This page has been left blank for your personal writings.)

FORGIVENESS JOURNAL

(This page has been left blank for your personal writings.)

FORGIVENESS JOURNAL

(This page has been left blank for your personal writings.)

FORGIVENESS JOURNAL

(This page has been left blank for your personal writings.)

FORGIVENESS JOURNAL

(This page has been left blank for your personal writings.)

FORGIVENESS JOURNAL

(This page has been left blank for your personal writings.)

FORGIVENESS JOURNAL

(This page has been left blank for your personal writings.)

Forgiveness Journal

(This page has been left blank for your personal writings.)

FORGIVENESS JOURNAL

(This page has been left blank for your personal writings.)

FORGIVENESS JOURNAL

(This page has been left blank for your personal writings.)

Printed in Great Britain
by Amazon

29916108R00066

DRIVING FORCE

THE EVOLUTION OF THE CAR ENGINE

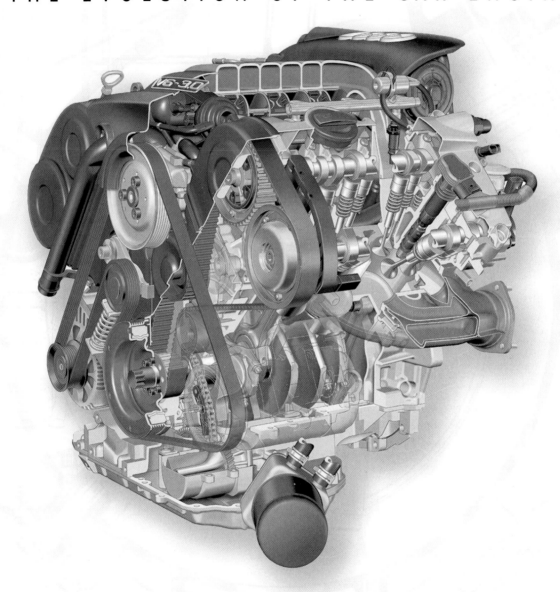

JEFF DANIELS

Haynes Publishing

First published in 2002

A catalogue record for this book is available from the British Library

ISBN 1 85960 877 9

Library of Congress catalog card no. 2002107498

Published by Haynes Publishing, Sparkford,
Yeovil, Somerset, BA22 7JJ, UK

Tel: 01963 442030 Fax: 01963 440001
Int. tel: +44 1963 442030 Int. fax: +44 1963 440001
E-mail: sales@haynes-manuals.co.uk
Web site: www.haynes.co.uk

Haynes North America, Inc.,
861 Lawrence Drive, Newbury Park,
California 91320, USA

Printed and bound in England by J. H. Haynes & Co. Ltd, Sparkford